RETREAT GUIDE

BLESSED ARE THE POOR IN SPIRIT

A RETREAT GUIDE ON THE FIRST BEATITUDE

FR. JOHN BARTUNEK, LC, STHD

This booklet is a part of RCSpirituality's *Retreat Guide* service, which includes free online videos and audio tracks available at **RCSpirituality.org**.

INTRODUCTION

RETREAT OVERVIEW

The Sermon on the Mount is St. Matthew's summary of Christ's preaching, of the New Law Jesus gives us from this mountain of the New Testament, just as Moses gave his people the Old Law on Mt. Sinai.

This New Law begins with the Beatitudes, the summary of the summary of Christ's teaching. The Beatitudes offer a portrait of Christian life, the only truly happy life (that's what "blessed"—"*beati*" in Latin, thus "beatitudes"—really means) we can have here on earth, the life that puts us on the sure path to heaven.

And the first characteristic of that portrait is this: "Blessed are the poor in spirit, for theirs is the kingdom of heaven" (Matthew 5:3). What does being "poor in spirit" really mean? What does it mean for you and me in today's world? It's worth digging into those questions, because we all ardently desire to inherit the kingdom of heaven, to enter into the fullness of life that comes from living in perfect communion with God. And digging into those questions is exactly what this Retreat Guide will do:

o The First Meditation explores the meaning of the words and how that meaning is clarified by Christ's own life, and by other biblical passages.

o The Second Meditation explores what this beatitude looked like in the life of one of history's most well known saints.

o The Conference gets practical by showing how we can grow in the virtues required by poverty of spirit.

Let's begin, in the quiet of our hearts, by turning our attention to God, who never stops paying attention to us. Let's ask him for all the graces we need, and most especially for the grace to understand a bit more clearly and to live a bit more fully the first Beatitude, blessed are the poor in spirit.

NOTES

FIRST MEDITATION

Living Life to the Full

INTRODUCTION

When Jesus declared the poor in spirit blessed, he wasn't inventing something completely new. Throughout the Old Testament, the truly fulfilling life is always associated with humbly and gratefully recognizing one's need for God. That's the essence of being poor in spirit: accepting the simple truth that apart from God, separated from God, in opposition to God, no one can truly live life to the full.

THE FIRST BEATITUDE AND THE FIRST TEMPTATION

It is interesting to note that Jesus puts this Beatitude at the front of the list, because this was precisely where our first parents failed. The devil tempted Adam and Eve by falsely promising that they could become like gods themselves, convincing them to reject their human limitations:

> But the serpent said to the woman, "You will not surely die. For God knows that when you eat of it your eyes will be opened, and you will be like God, knowing good and evil.
>
> —Genesis 3:4–5

This was the original temptation, the source of original sin: striving to be self-sufficient, rebelling against our intrinsic dependence on God, refusing to accept the limitations—the poverty—of our human nature.

THE FREEDOM OF LIVING IN THE TRUTH

Poverty of spirit overflows in immense interior freedom, because it grounds us firmly in the truth. The truth is, we are not God. None of us is all-powerful, none of us is all-knowing, none of us is eternal. We didn't create ourselves. We didn't create the universe. We have received our existence and our nature from God. And for our existence to bring us meaning and fulfillment—the happiness, the blessedness we yearn for—we have to accept and satisfy the simple demands of that nature.

This is obvious when it comes to the material demands of our human nature—no one pretends not to need food, water, sleep, and shelter. But for some reason, it is less obvious when it comes to the spiritual demands of our nature: the laws of morality, for example, are as real as the laws of biology, but we tend to act as if they aren't. Prayer is as necessary for our spiritual flourishing as breathing is for our material flourishing, but we tend to consider it optional. The poor in spirit are as aware of their spiritual needs as they are of their material needs, and they are wise enough to take good care of both.

JESUS AND POVERTY OF SPIRIT

Jesus lived to the full the poverty of spirit he praises in the first Beatitude. It may seem strange to say so. After all, he himself is God, so how could he humbly accept his need for God? Isn't that a contradiction? Not when we remember that God is a Trinity. As the Second Person of the Trinity, the Word of God, Jesus receives everything from the Father, and his life is continual communion with the Father. Jesus expresses this over and over again in the Gospels, especially in the Gospel of John. In one of his discussions with the Pharisees, he puts it like this:

So Jesus said (to them), "When you lift up the Son of Man, then you will realize that I AM, and that I do nothing on my own, but I say only what the Father taught me. The one who sent me is with me. He has not left me alone, because I always do what is pleasing to him.

—John 8:28–29

And towards the end of the Last Supper, he puts it like this:

I will no longer speak much with you, for the ruler of the world is coming. He has no power over me, but the world must know that I love the Father and that I do just as the Father has commanded me. Get up, let us go.

—John 14:23–24, 30–31

Jesus leans on the Father; he does nothing apart from the Father; his entire existence flows from and back to the Father. This is the very nature of God himself. As a Trinity of three divine persons in one divine nature, God lives from all eternity in perpetual mutual interdependence. Since we were created in God's own image and likeness, the deepest truth of our being mirrors that essential truth about God. Poverty of spirit is the recognition and acceptance of this truth, the truth that we are "made to live in communion with God, in whom we find happiness," as the Catechism puts it (#45).

GOING HOME JUSTIFIED

Jesus left us two parables illustrating, through contrast, this poverty of spirit that opens our hearts to God's grace. Both are from the Gospel of Luke. The first is a parable Jesus used to show how self-centered pride simply wraps us up so entirely in ourselves that it cuts us off from intimacy with God:

𝓕 He then addressed this parable to those who were convinced of their own righteousness and despised everyone else. "Two people went up to the temple area to pray; one was a Pharisee and the other was a tax collector. The Pharisee took up his position and spoke this prayer to himself, 'O God, I thank you that I am not like the rest of humanity—greedy, dishonest, adulterous—or even like this tax collector. I fast twice a week, and I pay tithes on my whole income.' But the tax collector stood off at a distance and would not even raise his eyes to heaven but beat his breast and prayed, 'O God, be merciful to me a sinner.' I tell you, the latter went home justified, not the former; for everyone who exalts himself will be humbled, and the one who humbles himself will be exalted.

—Luke 18:9–14

The tax collector recognized his own brokenness and sinfulness. He recognized that he needed God's mercy and grace, and he went to the Temple to humbly ask God for them.

This is our condition. We exist only because God holds us in existence. We have hope for fulfillment only because God has promised us his mercy and friendship. All that we are and all that we hope for is a gift flowing from God's goodness. Poverty of spirit opens us to receive that gift and thereby live it to the full.

The Pharisee, contrary to appearances, is actually unaware of his need for God. He is inflated with arrogance, convinced that he has made himself worthy of God, that he has made himself holy and righteous. He has completely forgotten the origin of his life, his knowledge, and his talents: he is blind to the gifts and the love of God.

A RICH FOOL

Another parable offers a stark representation of the foolishness that can come from worldly wealth, which so easily leads us to forget about our limitations and our true existential dependence on God:

❝Then he told them a parable. "There was a rich man whose land produced a bountiful harvest. He asked himself, 'What shall I do, for I do not have space to store my harvest?' And he said, 'This is what I shall do: I shall tear down my barns and build larger ones. There I shall store all my grain and other goods and I shall say to myself, "Now as for you, you have so many good things stored up for many years, rest, eat, drink, be merry!"' But God said to him, 'You fool, this night your life will be demanded of you; and the things you have prepared, to whom will they belong?' Thus will it be for the one who stores up treasure for himself but is not rich in what matters to God.

—Luke 12:16–21

For this man, the meaning of life was to be found in the accumulation of worldly wealth and honors, in what his own smarts and efforts could produce. He worked hard, but he was seduced by his success to the point where he completely forgot about the basic truth that earthly life doesn't last forever, and so the goods of this world cannot ultimately fulfill the deepest yearnings of our hearts.

HUMILITY, TRUTH, AND WISDOM

Poverty of spirit is humility, it is truth, it is the wisdom that sees the world as it truly is: a place of pilgrimage meant to lead us into a growing and everlasting friendship with God. And that is why the poor in spirit are blessed—theirs truly is the kingdom of heaven, because they never abandon the journey of faith to take up permanent residence in any merely passing kingdom of this wonderful but fleeting world.

In the next meditation, we will look at poverty of spirit in the life of St. Francis of Assisi. But for now, let's take some time, in the quiet of our hearts, to prayerfully reflect on the beauty, the wisdom, and the freedom that comes from poverty of spirit.

QUESTIONS FOR PERSONAL REFLECTION/GROUP DISCUSSION

1. When have I most felt my own limitations? How did I respond?

2. In what ways does the culture I live in encourage me to "be like God" without actually giving priority to my relationship with God?

3. How do I feel when I consider the truth that I am dependent on God for everything, from my continued existence to my hope for lasting happiness? Why do I feel that way?

QUOTATIONS TO HELP YOUR PRAYER

With what shall I come before the LORD,
and bow before God most high?
Shall I come before him with burnt offerings,
with calves a year old?

Will the LORD be pleased with thousands of rams,
with myriad streams of oil?
Shall I give my firstborn for my crime,
the fruit of my body for the sin of my soul?

You have been told, O mortal, what is good,
and what the LORD requires of you:
Only to do justice and to love goodness,
and to walk humbly with your God.

—Micah 6:6–8

"Remain in me, as I remain in you. Just as a branch cannot bear fruit on its own unless it remains on the vine, so neither can you unless you remain in me. I am the vine, you are the branches. Whoever remains in me and I in him will bear much fruit, because without me you can do nothing. Anyone who does not remain in me will be thrown out like a branch and wither; people will gather them and throw them into a fire and they will be burned. If you remain in me and my words remain in you, ask for whatever you want and it will be done for you. By this is my Father glorified, that you bear much fruit and become my disciples. As the Father loves me, so I also love you. Remain in my love. If you keep my commandments, you will remain in my love, just as I have kept my Father's commandments and remain in his love.

—John 15:4–10

"For though the fig tree does not blossom,
and no fruit appears on the vine,
Though the yield of the olive fails
and the terraces produce no nourishment,
Though the flocks disappear from the fold
and there is no herd in the stalls,
Yet I will rejoice in the LORD
and exult in my saving God.

—Habakkuk 3:17–18

NOTES

SECOND MEDITATION

A Saint Shows Us the Way

INTRODUCTION

In the whole history of the Church, perhaps one saint stands out more than any other for the poverty of spirit praised by Jesus in the first Beatitude: St. Francis of Assisi.

Founder of the Franciscan Order, St. Francis also developed and popularized two Catholic devotions still prominent in the Church today: the Way of the Cross and the Christmas Nativity scene. St. Francis's fascination with these two devotions reveal what fascinated him most about Jesus himself—his poverty. Jesus, as the eternal Word of God, was divine, infinitely rich in God's own magnificence. And yet, in order to redeem us from sin, he left heaven behind and took on the lowly condition of a human being. He willingly made himself a helpless baby, fully dependent on the care and protection of Joseph and Mary. And later, through his Passion, he willingly accepted the painful humiliations of injustice, torture, and betrayal. Jesus truly made himself poor, so as to open the door for us to share in his divine abundance.

A PAULINE POVERTY

Our Lord's voluntary poverty fascinated St. Paul as well. In the Second Letter to the Corinthians, he sums up Christ's poverty in words that reflect St. Francis's spirituality like a mirror:

For you know the gracious act of our Lord Jesus Christ, that for your sake he became poor although he was rich, so that by his poverty you might become rich.

—2 Corinthians 8:9

In another passage, used annually throughout the liturgical celebration of Holy Week, Paul described Christ's poverty like this:

℟ Have among yourselves the same attitude that is
also yours in Christ Jesus,
Who, though he was in the form of God,
did not regard equality with God something to be
grasped.
Rather, he emptied himself,
taking the form of a slave,
coming in human likeness;
and found human in appearance,
he humbled himself,
becoming obedient to death, even death on
a cross.

—Philippians 2:5–8

St. Francis, the son of a successful Italian merchant who spent the early part of his youth extravagantly enjoying the privileges of wealth and influence, ended up forsaking not only his family inheritance, but even his father's blessing and affection, because he couldn't resist the call to follow Christ's example of "emptying himself" and "humbling himself."

A KNIGHT OF LADY POVERTY

Francis lived in the age of chivalry, when Christian knights would consecrate themselves to defending the defenseless and fighting for justice in the name of a beautiful lady. St. Francis, applying the principles of chivalry to the spiritual realm, chose Lady Poverty as his patron, and spent his life in a counter-cultural material poverty that freed his soul to live profoundly the poverty of spirit lauded by the first Beatitude.

Historians speculate about the origin of Francis's decision to depend utterly on God's providence: owning nothing, accumulating nothing, surviving solely upon alms while he spent his days preaching the Gospel of his poor Lord Jesus in word and deed and passed his nights sleeping on the ground in huts or caves. Although we have no definitive answers to that question, since Francis himself wrote little, we do know something of the sequence of events through which he gradually discovered his vocation.

TORN BETWEEN TWO WORLDS

Both he and his family hoped that his natural leadership qualities and his father's wealth would somehow combine to break Francis into the ranks of the aristocracy and win the honor of knighthood. To this end, the future saint joined the other young men of Assisi as they were caught up in the various military conflicts riddling the Italian peninsula at the time. But instead of glory in battle, Francis experienced only disappointment.

His first excursion led to capture and imprisonment in a miserable dungeon for a year. He began his captivity in good spirits, but his health failed him and by the time he was released and welcomed home, his family could barely recognize him. Later, having recovered, he set out on another campaign, only to return after just one day, sick again, and having been mysteriously discouraged either by some kind of vision or some internal resistance to the worldly exploits that used to attract him so powerfully.

In this period, he waffled between the life of privilege and popularity he and his family had always envisioned for him, and a newfound attraction to contemplation, solitude, and serving the poor.

Once, after liquidating without permission some of his father's merchandise in order to finance the reconstruction of the dilapidated church of San Damiano, he was once again thrown into prison. This time, however, it was his own father who locked him inside a windowless storeroom in the family house. Eventually, when his father left town on business, Francis escaped. From then on, he lived partly as a hermit in the countryside around Assisi, and partly as a beggar, even making a pilgrimage to Rome in search of light and strength to follow where his Lord, Christ, and his chosen Lady, Poverty, were leading him.

When he returned to Assisi, dressed in rags and worn out from his vigils and fastings, his fellow townspeople mocked and derided him. They pelted him with mud and stones and laughed at him as the rich young man who had gone insane. His own father, furiously disappointed at how ungratefully his son had squandered the family's honor, sued him for having unlawfully disposed of the family's property. In the end, Francis was ordered by the bishop to make restitution, which he did publicly, returning the money gained from the illegal sale, and stripping himself of the very clothes on his back in full view of the crowd gathered outside the bishop's residence as he exclaimed in a loud voice: "These clothes are not mine. They were given to me. Now I tell you all that I have a Father in heaven and none other."

FROM DISAPPOINTMENT TO ENLIGHTENMENT

One by one, the good things of this earth had revealed themselves to the young Francis as undependable, as unfulfilling. First his dreams of gallantry and glorious success in battle had collapsed into imprisonment and sickness. Then the power of wealth to bring prosperity and joy had betrayed him and divided his family. The very friends and companions of his carefree youth turned on him when they thought he had lost his mind. His own father invoked the law against him and publicly humiliated him, simply because he had tried to serve God and the poor.

It had been a hard school, and risky; many people faced with similar contradictions have fallen into cynicism or despair. But God's grace was at work in his heart, and by his mid-twenties Francis had learned to lean solely on God, to abandon himself completely to God's wisdom and goodness, to follow as closely as possible Christ himself, who had once explained to a would-be disciple: "Foxes have dens and birds of the sky have nests, but the Son of Man has nowhere to rest his head" (Luke 9:58).

BLESSED ARE THE POOR IN SPIRIT

The blessedness that Francis experienced as a result of learning how to be poor in spirit wasn't reserved only to himself. In his lifetime, the Franciscan Order grew more rapidly than any religious order ever had. Dramatic conversions, along with miracles, followed in the wake of Francis and his first companions. The Franciscan spirituality has continued to inspire saints in every subsequent generation and in every corner of the world. Still today, so many centuries later, the joyful witness of Franciscan friars and nuns continues to bring the light of the Gospel to rich and poor alike, throughout the globe.

In an age when the Church had become prosperous and powerful even in worldly terms, God inspired Francis to witness to the truth about poverty of spirit through a radical commitment to voluntary material poverty and mortification. Not all of us are called to live solely from begging and to sleep in caves, but every single one of us is indeed called to experience the blessedness that comes from humbly recognizing and joyfully accepting our utter dependence on God. If we do, we will be able to find, as St. Francis did, the smile of God in every sunbeam and every success, in every hardship and every humiliation, in every neighbor and every need. And when that happens, we will truly be able to say that the kingdom of heaven is ours.

In the conference, we will explore practical ways to grow in this poverty of spirit. But for now, let's take some time, in the quiet of our hearts, to prayerfully consider what God may want to say to us through St. Francis's example of being poor in spirit.

QUESTIONS FOR PERSONAL REFLECTION/GROUP DISCUSSION

1. What has God been trying to teach me through the unfolding events of my life? How have I been responding?

2. What are the dominant sins of the age and culture in which I am living right now? What does the Gospel have to say about them?

3. When have I experienced profound disappointment or painful rejection? How did I respond? What does God want to teach me through those experiences?

QUOTATIONS TO HELP YOUR PRAYER

❝Therefore I tell you, do not worry about your life, what you will eat [or drink], or about your body, what you will wear. Is not life more than food and the body more than clothing? Look at the birds in the sky; they do not sow or reap, they gather nothing into barns, yet your heavenly Father feeds them. Are not you more important than they? Can any of you by worrying add a single moment to your life-span? Why are you anxious about clothes? Learn from the way the wild flowers grow. They do not work or spin. But I tell you that not even Solomon in all his splendor was clothed like one of them. If God so clothes the grass of the field, which grows today and is thrown into the oven tomorrow, will he not much more provide for you, O you of little faith? So do not worry and say, 'What are we to eat?' or 'What are we to drink?' or 'What are we to wear?' All these things the pagans seek. Your heavenly Father knows that you need them all. But seek first the kingdom [of God] and his righteousness, and all these things will be given you besides. Do not worry about tomorrow;

tomorrow will take care of itself. Sufficient for a day is its own evil.

—Matthew 6:25–34

❝The beatitude we are promised confronts us with decisive moral choices. It invites us to purify our hearts of bad instincts and to seek the love of God above all else. It teaches us that true happiness is not found in riches or well-being, in human fame or power, or in any human achievement—however beneficial it may be—such as science, technology, and art, or indeed in any creature, but in God alone, the source of every good and of all love:

> [Quotation from Blessed Cardinal Newman] All bow down before wealth. Wealth is that to which the multitude of men pay an instinctive homage. They measure happiness by wealth; and by wealth they measure respectability. . . . It is a homage resulting from a profound faith . . . that with wealth he may do all things. Wealth is one idol of the day and notoriety is a second. . . . Notoriety, or the making of a noise in the world—it may be called "newspaper fame"—has come to be considered a great good in itself, and a ground of veneration.

—*Catechism of the Catholic Church*, 1723

❝Most High, all-powerful, all-good Lord, All praise is Yours, all glory, all honour and all blessings.

To you alone, Most High, do they belong, and no

mortal lips are worthy to pronounce Your Name.

Praised be You my Lord with all Your creatures,
especially Sir Brother Sun,
Who is the day through whom You give us light.
And he is beautiful and radiant with great
splendour,
Of You Most High, he bears the likeness.

Praised be You, my Lord, through Sister Moon
and the stars,
In the heavens you have made them bright,
precious and fair.

Praised be You, my Lord, through Brothers Wind
and Air,
And fair and stormy, all weather's moods,
by which You cherish all that You have made.

Praised be You my Lord through Sister Water,
So useful, humble, precious and pure.
Praised be You my Lord through Brother Fire,
through whom You light the night and he is
beautiful and playful and robust and strong.

Praised be You my Lord through our Sister,
Mother Earth
who sustains and governs us,
producing varied fruits with coloured flowers and
herbs.
Praise be You my Lord through those who grant
pardon for love of You and bear sickness and trial.

Blessed are those who endure in peace, By You Most High, they will be crowned.

Praised be You, my Lord through Sister Death, from whom no-one living can escape. Woe to those who die in mortal sin!
Blessed are they She finds doing Your Will.

No second death can do them harm. Praise and bless my Lord and give Him thanks,
And serve Him with great humility.

—*Canticle of the Sun*,
St. Francis of Assisi

NOTES

CONFERENCE

Becoming Poor in Spirit

INTRODUCTION

In the Meditations of this Retreat Guide we considered what Jesus meant when he declared that those who are poor in spirit are blessed, that the kingdom of God will be theirs. Being poor in spirit simply means humbly recognizing and joyfully accepting our absolute dependence on God, and our need for real communion with God in order to find the happiness we yearn for.

Most Christians would agree with the truth of that statement. And yet, few Christians seem to live with the depth of interior freedom and the intensity of spiritual joy exhibited by St. Francis of Assisi and other saints who lived poverty of spirit so fruitfully. How can we grow in poverty of spirit and gradually experience more fully the blessedness that comes with it? That's what this conference will address.

UPROOTING THE WEEDS

Spiritual growth always involves working simultaneously in two directions. If we compare our souls to a garden, as so many spiritual writers throughout history have done, we can understand those two directions easily. On the one hand, we need to uproot the weeds, any plants that don't produce the fruit we want, but steal the nutrients and choke off the growth of the good plants.

When it comes to poverty of spirit, the humility which recognizes our radical dependence on God and joyfully accepts the consequences of such dependence, the main weed is spiritual pride, the arrogance that wants to be self-sufficient in the pursuit of happiness and holiness.

UNRULY PRIDE IN ACHIEVEMENTS

The most basic form of this spiritual arrogance shows itself when we think that our achievements—understood as worldly success experienced through money, awards, or other kinds of recognition—will bring us the fulfillment we yearn for.

Rooting out this weed involves purifying our intention—the "why" behind the "what" of our activities. Having purity of intention means striving to do our best in everything we undertake out of a sincere desire to serve those around us as well as possible, and in that way to reflect God's love in this world.

We can tell that this weed of arrogance is growing when we feel resentment toward people who have more success than we do, when we feel sad in response to someone performing better than we are in our chosen activities, or when thirst for success and achievement leads to the neglect of basic duties like prayer, honesty, quality time with family, and balanced, humble care for our own basic human needs.

We can tell that our intention is pure when we are able to rejoice in the successes of others as much as we rejoice in our own, and when we wisely keep a healthy balance between the different sectors of our lives.

SUBTLE PRIDE IN PURSUING HOLINESS

But there is another, more subtle form of spiritual arrogance as well. This weed can grow deep roots before we even recognize its presence. It has to do with a tendency toward self-sufficiency in our efforts for spiritual growth. In this scenario, we have already overcome our tendency to think that fulfillment will result from worldly success, but we start to think that success in our pursuit of holiness is primarily up to our own efforts. This leads us to start piling on spiritual and ascetic commitments, sometimes even to the detriment of our health and our family relationships. We start designing our own crosses by indiscriminately introducing all kinds of sacrifices and fasting. We start thinking of growth in holiness as a self-help program: push these buttons and check these things off the list, and we will become saints. We lose sight of the central importance of simple friendship with God, and we turn our spiritual lives into a kind of training program for the spiritual Olympics.

This approach to spiritual growth is extremely attractive to some personalities, because it offers absolute clarity and a high level of control. But it ends up feeding the weed of self-sufficiency and leading, often, to spiritual burnout, existential frustration, and even moral catastrophe.

Uprooting this form of spiritual arrogance, this self-sufficiency in holiness, is not easy. The best tools are regular spiritual direction with a wise spiritual guide or confessor, healthy fellowship and mutual accountability with a small group of friends who are also intentionally pursuing holiness, and ongoing study about the spiritual life.

CULTIVATING THREE PLANTS

Pulling out the weed of spiritual pride, and keeping an eye on the garden so that weed doesn't come back, is the first way we can cultivate poverty of spirit. The second way is by nourishing the virtues—the good plants in the garden of our soul—that produce the fruit of poverty of spirit. The key virtues related to this first Beatitude are humility, generosity, and gratitude. Humility is the virtue at the very core of poverty of spirit. The word "humility" comes from a Latin word meaning "of the earth" or "grounded," from the root word humus, which simply means "earth." In the Bible's creation account, human beings were created from the clay of the earth, into which God breathed the breath of life. Humility, then, is this awareness of our limitations and also of our greatness, of our dependence on God and our call to glorify him through making something beautiful of our lives.

EXERCISING HUMILITY BY GROWING FAITH

We can foster growth in humility especially in two ways. First, through prayer, reflection, and study we can fill our minds with the truths of our faith. Faith is our acceptance of what God has revealed to us about the world, ourselves, and himself. God has revealed the deepest truths about our origin, the source of our happiness, our need for grace, his own love for us, and his providential care for us. Constantly nourishing these truths and striving to understand them more and more deeply helps us correct the skewed worldview—often called our "darkened intellect"—that comes to us through the consequences of original sin. When Jesus proclaimed that he is the "light of the world" (John 8:12), he was impressing upon us the importance of absorbing into our minds all that he taught.

Think about how much information, how many images and ideas, enter our minds each day. How many of them come from the Gospel, the Catechism, the writings of the saints, and the teachings of the Church? Our minds are constantly being bombarded by half-truths and actual falsehoods—about our true identity, our value and worth, the nature of the world around us, the purpose of life, and the source of happiness. Popular culture in a secular, post-Christian world surrounds us and seduces us with lies about these most important topics. Unless we intentionally and regularly counteract that darkness by filling our minds with the light of Christ, there is simply no way we can deepen our experience of interior freedom that comes from living in the truth at the core of poverty of spirit.

EXERCISING HUMILITY BY REACTING TO FAILURES

Nourishing our faith isn't the only way to grow in humility. Reacting calmly and with a sense of humor to our failures and frustrations is another way.

Whenever things don't work out the way we planned, the way we wanted, or the way we thought they should, we find ourselves face to face with the truth of our own limitations and our own inherent weakness: we are not God, and so we can't govern the universe, or even our own lives, as if we were all-knowing and all-powerful.

Finding ourselves face to face with our limitations is a golden—a platinum—spiritual opportunity. Our natural, fallen selves tend to react to those situations with anger, resentment, violence, discouragement, or some other self-referential emotion—all reactions stemming from this distorted sense of pride, of expectations that we should be able to figure everything out and work everything out just by thinking clearly and acting wisely. But in fact, even when we do our best (which we don't always do), things don't always go well. When they don't, we have a chance to recognize and joyfully accept the simple truth that we are not God. Here's how St. Paul described his own experience of the golden spiritual opportunity that presents itself to us every time we fail or fall or make a mistake:

> Therefore, that I might not become too elated, a thorn in the flesh was given to me, an angel of Satan, to beat me, to keep me from being too elated. Three times I begged the Lord about this, that it might leave me, but he said to me, "My grace is sufficient for you, for power is made perfect in weakness." I will rather boast most gladly of my weaknesses, in order that the power of Christ may dwell with me. Therefore, I am content with weaknesses, insults, hardships, persecutions, and constraints, for the sake of Christ; for when I am weak, then I am strong.
>
> —2 Corinthians 12:7–10

Whenever we experience our weakness, whether through failure or frustration, paying attention to our reaction to that experience, and steering that reaction toward calm confidence in God and a sense of humor regarding our own limitations, is a sure way of nourishing humility and cultivating the blessed fruit of poverty of spirit.

THE FREEDOM OF GENEROSITY

Generosity is another virtue that blossoms with the first Beatitude. Generosity is that beautiful capacity to share with others whatever we have. Generosity is the contrary of greed, which accumulates things and hoards things and takes a crooked pleasure in simply having more than other people. This starves the soul, feeding the weeds of self-sufficiency and arrogance. Generosity—with our money, our goods, our time, our attention—frees the soul. The joyful Scrooge at the end of Charles Dickens's A Christmas Carol is someone who has weeded out greedy miserliness through acts of generosity. Only the generous person will avoid the spiritual snares and tangles that come from setting our hearts on material possessions. This is why Jesus could say to his disciples,

Amen, I say to you, it will be hard for one who is rich to enter the kingdom of heaven. Again I say to you, it is easier for a camel to pass through the eye of a needle than for one who is rich to enter the kingdom of God.

—Matthew 19:23–24

Material goods—wealth, honor, even knowledge and experience, in a certain sense—are not bad in themselves. But because of the twisted tendencies of our fallen human nature, we have a penchant for becoming inordinately attached to things that we own. That attachment undermines our poverty of spirit by feeding a false sense of self-sufficiency, and even convincing us that our true happiness is somehow more dependent on material prosperity than on communion with God. Generosity, giving or sharing our goods, whatever they may be, with those in need, not only gives us a chance to live Christ's commandment of love, but also protects us from the stranglehold of greed.

THE COMMON-SENSE WISDOM OF ASCETICISM

Being temperate in our use of material goods is an excellent means for encouraging generosity. This involves disciplining our desires for luxury and indulgence—again, not because the good things of the earth are evil, but simply because, due to our fallen nature, it is extremely easy for us to become inordinately attached to these things.

In this sense, the Church's own liturgical rhythm of feast days and fast days can be of great assistance. Celebrating feast days and Sundays with family and friends, with good food and healthy entertainment and recreation, is a healthy way to enjoy material things. Creatively putting some self-imposed limits on our use of material goods on other days—for example: taking a cold shower, drinking only water at meals, eating less than we would like, abstaining from certain forms of entertainment, faithfully exercising, and doing chores—these kinds of small sacrifices can be a healthy way to keep an eye on our fallen nature.

This is what the Catholic spiritual tradition refers to as asceticism or voluntary renunciation: a balanced, common-sense vigilance over the disordered tendencies at work in our fallen human nature. It keeps us free to be generous, and that in turn nourishes our poverty of spirit.

THE POWER OF GRATITUDE

Finally, poverty of spirit receives a real boost from one of the most beautiful expressions of humility: namely, gratitude. A grateful person simply cannot fall into self-sufficiency. A grateful person acknowledges our dependence on God's goodness and power, manifested either directly or through the generosity of others. A grateful person knows how to accept gifts joyfully. This implies a humble acceptance of one's own needs, of one's limitations, and of the goodness of other people—all signs of poverty of spirit, all contrary to spiritual pride, arrogance, and diabolical self-sufficiency. A proud person may accept a gift joyfully, but only because that person thinks he or she deserves it. That is not gratitude. It doesn't establish a real connection with the giver, a real interpersonal relationship.

Gratitude can be lived intentionally in our relationships with other people, but it can also be lived intentionally in our relationship with God. In fact, the most perfect prayer and act of worship in the world, the Sacrifice of the Mass, is known as the Celebration of the Eucharist, and the word Eucharist means "thanksgiving." By offering to God the very Body and Blood of Christ, united to ourselves through humble prayer and sacramental communion, we are showing how grateful we are for the very gift God has given us in Christ. Nothing is more precious to us than our communion with Jesus, and so we have nothing more precious to offer God in thanksgiving for his grace than our very selves united to our Lord.

The more we can weave gratitude into our prayer, not just asking God for all the things we need, but taking time to thank him for all his gifts and to savor those gifts, the more we nourish the poverty of spirit that allows for deeper communion with our Creator and Redeemer. The more time and space we make to experience God's goodness as manifested through his giving us so many gifts, the more our souls rejoice in discovering how deeply we are known, loved, and valued by the Lord. That discovery leads us out of the darkness of this fallen world and into the light of God's kingdom. For those reasons, gratitude is, as some spiritual writers have described it, the shortcut to holiness.

BEING GOOD GARDENERS

Cultivating poverty of spirit involves uprooting (and keeping uprooted) the weeds of spiritual pride, as well as nourishing the virtues of humility (through bolstering our faith and keeping an eye on how we react to failures and frustrations), generosity (including a healthy dose of asceticism), and gratitude. Blessed are we if we make a point of doing our part in that cultivation, for the kingdom of heaven will be ours.

Take some time now to prayerfully reflect on the questions in the personal questionnaire, which will help you apply these general truths to your personal circumstances.

PERSONAL QUESTIONNAIRE

1. What do I do to nourish my knowledge of my faith on a regular basis? What has most helped me grow in the knowledge of my faith in the past?

2. What more could I do in this area, in order to continue growing in my knowledge of the truth in a way that nourishes humility?

3. How often do I find myself getting stressed or worried about my spiritual growth? In what ways could this be a sign of spiritual pride and subtle spiritual self-sufficiency?

4. When do I most frequently find myself face to face with my limitations? What kinds of failures, disappointments, and frustrations do I most frequently have to deal with? How do I usually react to them?

5. Name someone I know who models humility in an attractive way for me. What makes it so attractive?

6. In what ways am I generous? In what ways am I ungenerous? How can I be more generous (with my money, time, expertise, attention…)? How is God asking me to be more generous?

7. Does healthy asceticism have any place in my life? How often do I purposely make small sacrifices in order to keep an eye on the disordered tendencies of my fallen nature?

8. Who in my experience is an attractive model of generosity and why?

9. How often do I find myself saying "thank you" to the people around me, especially the people close to me? Objectively speaking, should I be thanking them more frequently?

10. What place does gratitude have in my relationship with God, especially in my prayer life? How can I make it more present in my prayer life this week?

NOTES

FURTHER READING

If you feel moved to continue reflecting and praying about this theme, you may find the following books helpful:

Rejoice and Be Glad: Apostolic Exhortation on the Call to Holiness in Today's World
by Pope Francis

Seeking First the Kingdom: 30 Meditations on How to Love God with All Your Heart, Soul, Mind, and Strength
by Fr. John Bartunek, LC

Brother Francis: The Barefoot Saint of Assisi
by Paul McCusker (audio drama)

Back to Virtue
by Peter Kreeft

EXPLORING MORE

Please visit our website, *RCSpirituality.org,* for more spiritual resources, and follow us on Facebook for regular updates: *facebook.com/RCSpirituality.*

If you would like to support and sponsor a Retreat Guide, please consider making a donation at RCSpirituality.org.

Retreat Guides are a service of Regnum Christi.
RegnumChristi.org

Produced by Coronation Media.
CoronationMedia.com

Developed & Self-published by RCSpirituality.
RCSpirituality.org

Printed in Great Britain
by Amazon